The History Detective series
Tudor Home
Tudor Medicine
Tudor Theatre
Tudor War
Victorian Crime
Victorian Factory
Victorian School
Victorian Transport

First published in Great Britain in 2002 by Hodder Wayland,
an imprint of Hodder Children's Books
© Copyright 2002 Hodder Wayland
This paperback edition published in 2003

Hodder Children's Books
A division of Hodder Headline Limited
338 Euston Road, London NW1 3BH

Editor: Kay Barnham
Designer: Simon Borrough
Cartoon artwork: Richard Hook
Map illustration: Peter Bull
Picture research: Shelley Noronha – Glass Onion Pictures

British Library Cataloguing in Publication Data

Hepplewhite, Peter
    The history detective investigates Tudor war
    1. Military art and science – England – History –
    Juvenile literature
    2. Great Britain – History, Military – 1485-1603 –
    Juvenile literature
    I. Title II. Tudor war
    355'.02'0942'09031

ISBN 0 7502 3742 2

Printed and bound in Italy by G. Canale & C.S.p.A., Turin

Picture acknowledgements:
The publishers would like to thank the following for
permission to reproduce their pictures: The Art
Archive Limited 26 (top); The Board of Trustees of the
Armouries 1 and 6, 7 (top), 10 (left) and *cover*; The
Bridgeman Art Library 4 (right), 8 (bottom), 16 (top),
24 (top and bottom) and *cover*, 28, 29 (top); Martin
Chillmaid 8 (top); English Heritage Photo Library 18,
19 (top and bottom); Fotomas Index 14, 17; Hodder
Wayland Picture Library 26 (bottom); The Hulton
Deutsch Collection 9; Mary Evans Picture Library 4
(left) and *cover*, 5 and *cover*, 10 (bottom), 11, 12 13
(left), 15 (top and bottom), 22 (right), 23, 27, 29; The
Mary Rose Trust 20 and *cover*, 21; National Trust
Photographic Library 25 (top) (Andrew Butler);
Oxford Scientific Films 22 (left) Larry Crowhurst, 22
(top left) (Colin Milkins); The Public Record Office 7
(bottom); Tullie House Museum, Carlisle 16.

THE HISTORY DETECTIVE INVESTIGATES

or War

Hepplewhite

HODDER
Wayland

An imprint of Hodder Children's Books

Contents

How did the Tudors win the throne of England?

The history detective Sherlock Bones, will help you to find clues and collect evidence about Tudor wars – what they were like and what it was like to fight in them. Wherever you see one of Sherlock's paw-prints, you will find a mystery to solve. The answers can be found on pages 30 and 31.

The Tudors ruled England from 1485–1601. Being an English king or queen was a dangerous job. The first Tudor monarch, Henry VII, won the throne at the Battle of Bosworth in 1485. However, what had been taken by force could be lost by force. Every Tudor sovereign depended upon the loyalty of the army and navy to fight enemies at home and abroad.

In August 1485, Henry Tudor, then Earl of Richmond, landed his small army at Milford Haven in Wales. He was a young rebel, eager to seize the throne. He marched north through Wales and called on his supporters to join him. The king, Richard III, summoned his armies and caught Henry at Bosworth Field in Leicestershire. Two hours of bitter fighting later, Richard was dead. England had a new king, Henry VII.

The Battle of Bosworth was the last battle in the Wars of the Roses. Henry VII belonged to the Lancaster family, whose emblem was the red rose. Richard III belonged to the York family, whose emblem was the white rose. The leaders of these two powerful families had been fighting for more than thirty years over who should be king.

Henry was born and brought up in Wales. He was very proud of his Welsh ancestors.

Why did Henry VII have a red dragon in his emblem?

DETECTIVE WORK

Find out how many English kings and queens had to fight to hold on to their kingdoms. Draw a timeline called England's Deadly Throne. Start in 1066 with William the Conqueror. This website will help you – www.royal.gov.uk

An Italian historian described how Henry was lucky to win at Bosworth against such a brave enemy:

Richard learned that Henry was some way off, with only a few armed men as his escort... Inflamed with anger he spurred his horse and rode against him... In the first charge Richard killed several men and toppled Henry's standard, along with the standard bearer William Brandon. Then behold William Stanley came in with 3,000 men to support Henry. Richard was slain in the thickest of the fighting.

Polydore Vergil, 1510

The Battle of Bosworth was very fierce and bloody.

How did people become soldiers?

In 1485, armies were formed as they had been for centuries. The king issued a *Commission of Array* – an order to the great noblemen to join him with bands of soldiers that they had recruited and paid for themselves. This was fine if the nobles feared the king, but if not, they might fight against him. Henry VII knew that some lords had become too powerful during the Wars of the Roses and he banned them from keeping their own private armies.

To find new ways of raising troops, the Tudors turned to the militia. The militia were part-time soldiers organized by the Lord Lieutenant and magistrates of the county. The soldiers trained for only a few days each year. This training session was called the summer 'muster'.

Bristling with weapons, an English army marches through Ireland.

A sixteenth-century 'pot' helmet.

In each county all men between 16 and 60 had to be ready to defend their home area. Ordinary workers had to turn out, equipped with their own 'pot' helmet and weapon. The richest nobles, worth £1,000 a year or more, had to supply 16 horses, 80 suits of armour, 40 pikes, 30 bows, 20 muskets and 50 'pots' (helmets).

The militia could not be ordered to serve abroad, so armies fighting in Europe had to be raised from volunteers. Usually there were enough men looking for adventure and loot, but sometimes soldiers had to be forced to join up.

Captain Barnaby Rich was a soldier during Elizabeth I's reign (1558–1603). He described how some men were recruited to fight:

Every petty constable of every parish must bring two or three able-bodied men.
The constable is loth that any honest man should hazard himself amongst the many dangers of war, wherefor if there hap to be any idle fellow, drunkard, quarreller – or such a one as hath some skill in stealing a goose – these shall be presented to the service of the prince.

❖ Do you think recruits like those described by Barnaby Rich would make good soldiers?

A Tudor muster roll

DETECTIVE WORK

Many historic towns had a Tudor militia. Ask your local library or archive if they have a 'muster roll' (like the one below). See who could be called on to defend their town and what weapons they had to bring.

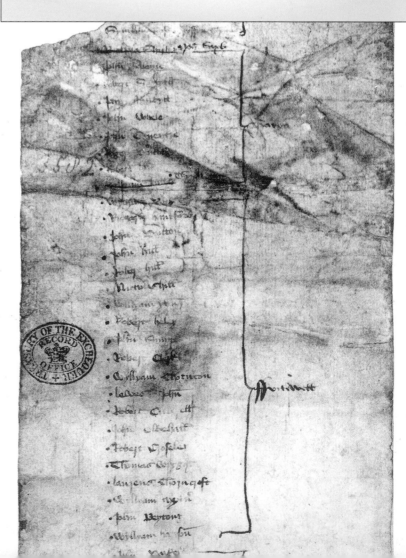

What was it like to be a Tudor soldier?

There were many different types of soldier in Tudor times. From left to right, you can see a musketeer, an archer and a bill-man.

The engraving below shows a Tudor soldier firing a cannon.

For most of the sixteenth century, the best armies in Europe were Spanish or French. English armies were not nearly as good. However, during the reign of Elizabeth I, from 1558 to 1603, there were long wars in the Netherlands and Ireland. English troops had to become more experienced – or lose every battle.

Under Elizabeth I, over 80,000 soldiers were trained and sent to fight abroad – out of a population of only 4 million. Some had been forced to join up and looked for the first chance to desert, or run away. To stop this happening, new recruits were marched from their home parish to camp under the stern eyes of officers.

Tudor soldiers served in companies of about a hundred men, each led by a captain. The captain was not just an officer – he was also a businessman. He trained his men, led them in battle and supplied their weapons, uniforms, food and wages. To make a profit, he hired his company to the government. Most captains were dishonest and claimed 'dead-pays' – money for soldiers who had died.

Conditions in the army could be appalling. More men died of plague and sickness than died fighting. In 1591, for example, the Earl of Essex led an army of 3,600 men to attack Normandy, in France. Soon, all but 800 were too ill to fight or had died from disease. Faced with such risks, it is not surprising that soldiers looked forward to their beer ration. For troops fighting in the Netherlands, this was four pints a day. In Ireland, where the weather was wetter, the ration was two pints of beer and half a pint of whiskey.

Since pay was poor, soldiers believed they had the right to steal from the enemy and nearby civilians. This Irish cartoon shows an English soldier laden with plunder.

❀ Can you suggest reasons why the beer ration was so generous?

A soldier's pay in the army of Queen Elizabeth was described by one historian:

There are sixteen thousand footmen, distributed into 160 bands, each band having a captain at four shillings a day, a lieutenant at two shillings a day, an ensign at 18 pence a day, two sergeants, a drummer and a surgeon, each at twelve pence a day, and 94 soldiers at eight pence a day.

Fynes Moryson, *Itinerary*, 1598

What weapons did Tudor soldiers use?

Tudor soldiers were armed with many lethal weapons. Some, such as daggers and bows and arrows, had not changed since the Middle Ages. Others, such as handguns, were new inventions. All were very dangerous.

Most of the nobles in Tudor armies wore armour and charged into battle on horseback. Because armour was so expensive, it was passed down from father to son. The best armour was imported from Germany or Italy. It had curved surfaces to deflect arrows and blows from other weapons.

Nobles' favourite weapons were the sword or lance. Most Tudor soldiers were infantry – foot soldiers who trained with different weapons and marched into battle.

Archers were the deadliest soldiers in early Tudor times. Their longbows, made from yew, could put an arrow through a solid oak door 8 cm thick.

This impressive suit of armour is now displayed at the Tower of London.

Archers carried about fifty arrows and could fire them all in minutes, shattering an enemy attack.

Their bows and arrows are thicker than those used by other nations, just as their arms are stronger, for they seem to have hands and arms of iron. As a result their bows have as long a range as our crossbows.

Italian priest, Dominic Mancini, visiting England in 1482–3

Hand-gunners brought a new smell to Tudor battlefields – the bad-egg stink of gunpowder. Early handguns were called arquebuses, which made a lot of noise and smoke. However, they had a range of barely 100 m and were very inaccurate. But, by 1600, larger and heavier muskets had improved so much that no modern army could hope to win a battle without plenty of musketeers (soldiers who fired muskets).

Pike-men used pikes – spears with very long shafts – up to 5.5 m long. Formations of pike-men were used to stop cavalry charges.

Bill-men fought with bills. These weapons had heads shaped like spears, hooks and axes all in one. They were fitted to a long shaft for stabbing horsemen.

🐾 It took years of practice to make a good bowman. Why do you think it took so long?

This musketeer is loading gunpowder into his gun.

DETECTIVE WORK

Ask your local museum if they have any fifteenth- or sixteenth-century weapons. How big and heavy are they? How would a soldier use them? Sketch and describe them and make a display.

What was it like to fight in a battle?

The Battle of Flodden was the bloodiest in Britain during Tudor times. It was fought on 9 September 1513 between England and Scotland. James IV, the Scottish king, invaded England with an army of 35,000. The English militia was called out and 26,000 men gathered at Newcastle. Led by the Earl of Surrey, they challenged James to battle on a bleak Northumberland moor. The fighting was a disaster for Scotland. James was killed – and half of the Scottish nobility died with him.

Flodden was fought on a cold, wet afternoon just before dusk. English cannon knocked out the Scottish guns and smashed into the enemy infantry for over an hour. Iron cannonballs ripped through the Scottish army, blasting men to pieces.

✿ What weapons can you see in the picture below?

Old enemies, England and Scotland, fought against each other in the Battle of Flodden.

Unable to stand this any longer, the Scottish attacked. Most were armed with long pikes and they had taken off their shoes to get a better grip in the muddy fields. Bristling like a hedgehog the Scottish army advanced. But the English had better weapons. Using their shorter bills like axes, they could cut the heads off the enemy pikes.

Flodden then became a bitter hand-to-hand fight. The Scots threw away their useless pikes and took out swords and daggers. Men hacked, slashed and stabbed at each other until they were exhausted. The mud turned red with blood. Few prisoners were taken and no mercy was shown. James IV died like a hero: he slew five Englishmen with his pike before it broke in his hands. The Scots lost 9,000 troops and the English 4,000.

A tired, beaten soldier returns home after the Battle of Flodden.

✕ battle
✳ rebellion

Tudor battles and rebellions in Britain

① Flodden, Northumberland   1513
② Solway Moss, near Carlisle   1542
③ Pinkie, near Musselburgh   1547
④ The Pilgrimage of Grace   1536
⑤ The Western Rebellion   1549
⑥ Kett's Rebellion   1549
⑦ Wyatt's Rebellion   1554
⑧ The Northern Rebellion   1569

DETECTIVE WORK

The site of the Battle of Flodden is now popular with tourists. Find out if there are any historical battle sites that you can visit in your area. Ask your nearest Tourist Information Office or local studies library.

What happened to wounded soldiers?

Tudor battles left many soldiers hideously injured. Pikes, bills and swords made deep puncture wounds, while arrowheads had large barbs (spikes) that tore the flesh when they were pulled out.

Treatment given by battlefield surgeons could be skilful. But new weapons brought new problems. Firearms caused injuries that often led to an arm or leg being amputated. Worse still for the poor patients, surgeons were taught to burn wounds to stop the bleeding and prevent infection. They did this with boiling oil or red-hot irons.

This illustration from one of surgeon William Clowes' books shows battle scenes and some of the instruments he used.

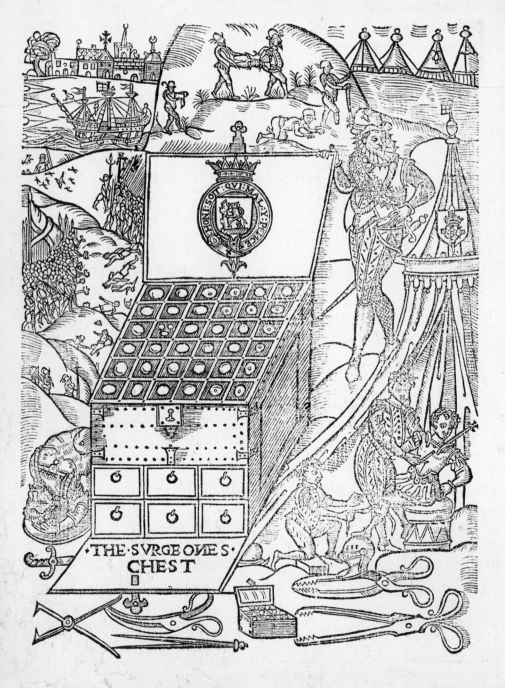

·THE·SVRGEONES· CHEST

One of the greatest surgeons of the day was a Frenchman – Ambroise Paré. He was horrified by cruel treatments and looked for better methods. He recommended using ligatures (cords) to tie up the ends of arteries after a limb had been amputated. Although many doctors thought his ideas were ridiculous, the English surgeon William Clowes knew they made sense. He treated sailors wounded in the battle against the Spanish Armada in 1588, and wrote the first account in English of Paré's techniques.

✿ Why do you think battles have been called the classrooms of surgeons?

Ambroise Paré spoke of new treatments for amputees:

When you have cut off the member (limb), let it bleed a little to prevent inflammation. Then let the veins and arteries be bound (tied) up as speedily as you can so that the course of the flowing blood may be stopped.
Verily I confess I used to use various hot irons on the dismembered part. This was a thing of great horror, bringing torment to the patient. I must earnestly beg all Chirurgions (surgeons) to leave this old and too cruel way of healing.

1536

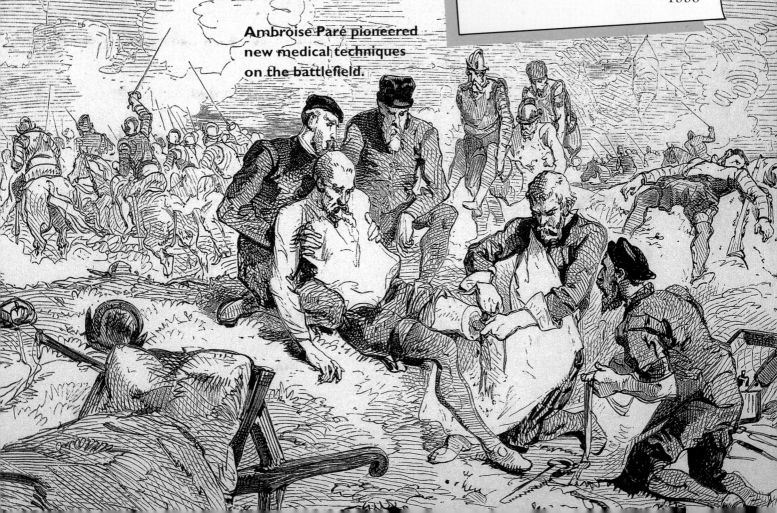

Ambroise Paré pioneered new medical techniques on the battlefield.

Where was the most dangerous place in Tudor Britain?

The Keeper of Liddesdale tried to enforce the law from Hermitage Castle, this lonely fortress in one of the most violent dales in the Borders.

*I*f there was one place to avoid in Tudor Britain, it was the area called the Border Marches between England and Scotland. The 175-kilometre frontier was a wild land controlled by clans of cattle thieves and murderers – the dreaded Border Reivers.

The Border Marches had been a fierce battleground for almost 300 years and the people who lived there had become hardened to war. Like modern gangsters they made a living out of violence – robbery, protection rackets, raiding, feuding and killing became a way of life. Cut-throat families such as the Armstrongs, Elliotts and Kerrs could even raise their own small armies, sometimes hundreds strong.

DETECTIVE WORK

Are you from a family of thieves and villains? To find out more about the Border Reivers' family names, visit this website: www.northumberland.gov.uk/VG/rvintro.html

In the summer of 1581, the Elliots from Scotland raided the West March of England (now Cumbria). They stole 274 cattle and 12 horses, ransacked nine houses, wounded three men and took one prisoner. But this was nothing special – just a routine attack by one of the dozens of families causing mayhem in the Borders every year.

This behaviour could only go on because the Reivers played England and Scotland off against one another – siding first with one country, then the other. The Wardens of the Marches struggled to keep law and order, but some were part-time bandits themselves! Others, who were honest, died in the attempt. In 1575, Sir George Heron, Keeper of Tynedale, was murdered at a wardens' meeting!

✤ Look up the word *reiver* in a dictionary. What does it mean?

✤ Now look up *blackmail*. This was a word that the Border Reivers gave to the English language. What does it mean?

The Border Reivers came raiding on horseback, armed with leather jackets, steel helmets, lances and bows.

A Tudor bishop described the Border Reivers' night raids:

They sally out in the night in troops, through remote by-ways. All the day time they hide in lurking holes till they arrive in the dark at those places they have a design on... The more skilful any captain is to pass through those wild places, crooked turnings and deep precipices, in the thickest mists, his reputation is the greater.

Leslie, Bishop of Ross, 1549

What kind of forts did the Tudors build?

The largest of Henry VIII's coastal forts was in Deal, Kent. Built 1539–40, it had 145 gun-ports so that cannon could defend against attacks from the sea.

*I*n 1534, Henry VIII made himself head of the Protestant Church of England. After this, there was always the risk of invasion by the most powerful Catholic countries – France and Spain. To the king's shock, the worst almost happened in 1545, when French troops landed on the Isle of Wight.

To protect the south coast, Henry built a chain of forts from Kent to Cornwall – the first modern scheme of national defence. These strongholds were completely different from the medieval castles dotted across the English countryside. The power and range of Tudor cannon meant that the high walls and towers of older castles did not shield against attack.

With the danger from enemy guns in mind, Henry hired a German architect – Stefan van Haschenperg. Stefan saw to it that the new forts were based on up-to-date ideas from Europe – walls were low and thick, protecting round artillery platforms. Inside were bronze or iron cannon, mounted on wheeled carriages. They could be moved to fire from any gun-port.

Henry VIII loved the 'exceedingly great noyse and marvellous rore' of artillery. To avoid buying these from abroad, the king set up the Ordnance Department, the oldest permanent military department in the British Army. His new forts were soon equipped with cannon made in gun foundries in Sussex.

A new shape of fort became popular during Elizabeth I's reign. The arrow-headed bastion's pointed shape made Henry VIII's forts seem old-fashioned. The walls were made of packed earth, faced with stone, to absorb the impact of powerful cannonballs.

Pendennis Castle is an example of an arrow-headed bastion.

DETECTIVE WORK

Compare the design of a medieval castle with a Tudor fort. Make your own drawings to show how the threat of cannon changed the design of the different strongholds.

The huge Tudor cannon below is now on view at Dover Castle. It is nicknamed 'Queen Elizabeth's pocket pistol'.

☙ Why do you think the cannon was given this nickname?

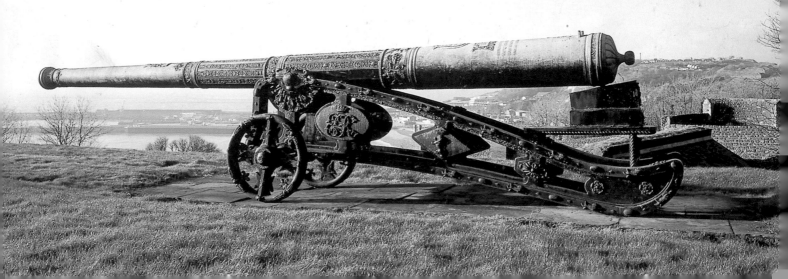

How did people become sailors?

In Tudor times, sailors were England's first line of defence. Historians agree that the modern navy began during the reign of Henry VIII. But there had been impressive English navies before this. What was now different?

DETECTIVE WORK

Visit the Mary Rose website: www.maryrose.org/ to find out more about 'the only sixteenth-century warship on display anywhere in the world'.

Built 1509–10, the *Mary Rose* was a magnificent Tudor warship.

The constant threat of invasion meant that England needed a large fleet. Records from 1548 show that at least fifty-two vessels were ready for action. However, the back-up was as important as the warships. New dockyards and storehouses were built on the Thames at Deptford, Woolwich and Chatham, as well as along the south coast. But most importantly, the Navy Board was set up in 1546. This organization employed well-paid officials who knew about ships and the sea. It paved the way for a full-time navy.

It was difficult for the navy to find enough sailors to work for them. Some seamen, who worked on fishing boats or merchant ships, volunteered to join the navy. In times of emergency, however, the government needed to order many more men to join up. But, the navy did not pay well and the best sailors often joined privateers instead. These were licensed pirate ships, with crews hoping to make their fortunes by capturing or looting enemy vessels.

What stores and equipment do you think that a Tudor warship would need to stay shipshape and fighting fit? Make a list.

The *Mary Rose* sank in the Solent in 1545. In 1982, in one of the great adventures of archaeology she was raised from the seabed in a giant cradle.

What was it like to be a Tudor sailor?

Weevils and maggots often ruined the sailors' food before they could eat it.

Life on board a Tudor warship was hard, and the crew had to be young and fit. Most were under 30. In 1545, a large ship like the *Mary Rose* needed around 200 sailors, but also carried 185 soldiers and 30 gunners. Sailors were paid very low wages and when they were laid off at the end of a war, they had no pensions to look forward to. The best an injured or sick seaman could expect was a licence to beg.

A sailor's diet was no better than his wages. Meals were made from foods that had been preserved for long voyages: salted beef and pork; dried cod; and dried peas. Instead of bread, sailors ate biscuit – softened with beer!

❀ Sailors often had maggots in their food. What do you think they tasted like?

This modern painting shows a Tudor sailor who is ready for war.

Sometimes, sailors' 'victuals', or meals, were rotten when the storage casks were opened. In 1599, Vice-Admiral Lord Thomas Howard complained:

Both our fish and beef is so corrupt as it will destroy all the men we have if they feed on it but a few days.

This cartoon shows some of the harsh punishments used aboard ship. Thieves were dunked three times in the sea and put off the ship at the nearest port.

Scurvy – an illness caused by lack of vitamins – was common and caused the death of around 10,000 sailors during the reign of Queen Elizabeth. Seamen also faced many other diseases, including typhus, dysentery and plague. Many sailors survived fierce battles only to die of disease soon afterwards.

DETECTIVE WORK

Find out about pay and conditions in the Royal Navy today. The Navy website: www.royal-navy.mod.uk/ is a good place to start.

Sickness and mortality begins wonderfully to grow among us... The Elizabeth Jonas hath had a great infection in her... of the 500 men which she carried... there were dead of them 200 and above. I was driven to set the rest of her men ashore and to make fires in her of wet broom three or four days together and so hoped to have cleansed her of infection.

Lord Howard of Effingham, Commander of the English Fleet, 1588.

Who was England's most famous sailor?

Sir Francis Drake.

Tudor England had a number of brilliant navy commanders. One of the most successful was Sir Francis Drake, who lived during the reign of Elizabeth I. He played an important role in the battle against the Armada – a fleet of Spanish warships.

Francis Drake was born into a poor family in Devon, around 1541–3. He was the eldest of twelve brothers. Drake's humble background made him envious of those who were born nobles.

After serving as a sailor's apprentice, Drake sailed with his cousin to sell slaves to Spanish settlements in the West Indies. The English ships were attacked and all but two destroyed. Drake lost a fortune and returned home with a bitter hatred of the Spanish.

♣ Drake chose the motto *Sic Parvis Magna*. Using the Internet, find out what this means. Why do you think he chose these words?

A map showing Drake's route when he sailed around the world and the Spanish Empire.

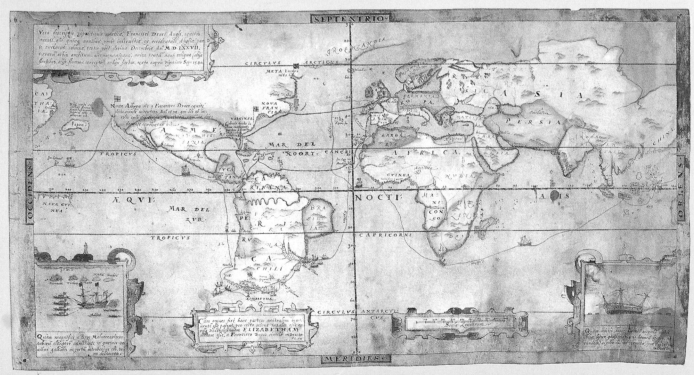

DETECTIVE WORK

Read the poem *Drake's Drum* by Sir Henry Newbolt. You can find it in poetry anthologies and on the Internet. Track down the creepy legends of the drum. Will Drake rise to save England in your lifetime?

Buckland Abbey, the house and small estate that Drake bought with Spanish loot. This was his signal to the world that he had 'made it'.

Between 1577 and 1580, Drake made the first English voyage around the world. When he returned, his ship – *the Golden Hinde* – was loaded with plunder from Spanish ships and colonies in the Americas. His voyage had the secret support of Queen Elizabeth; her share of the treasure was £400,000 – and Drake was knighted.

In 1587, Drake attacked and burnt Spanish ships in Cadiz and delayed the Armada for a year. The following year, he was made vice-admiral of the fleet and played a leading part in the battles against the Armada (see pages 26–27). Drake did not like taking orders and some in government thought him common and unreliable. But he became a brave and inspiring leader who earned the respect of his crews. Sir Francis Drake's bold attacks on the Spanish made him a national hero.

How did England defeat the Spanish Armada?

*I*n July 1588, the fearsome Spanish Armada set sail. The Catholic King Philip II of Spain had finally decided to crush Protestant England with a fleet of warships. The Spanish planned to sweep aside the English navy, pick up extra troops from Calais, in France, and invade England, where they would crush the English militia. But it all went horribly wrong.

The Armada was led by the Duke of Medina Sidonia. He had no experience of commanding ships and believed the invasion plan was bound to fail. Lord Howard of Effingham and Sir Francis Drake, experienced and confident sailors, were in charge of the English navy.

Although the Armada had around 140 ships, only about 20 of these were warships. The English fleet was around 120 strong, but about 30 of these were galleons – faster and better armed than most Spanish vessels.

The English galleons were sleek, easy to manoeuvre and carried heavy bronze or iron cannon. They were good for short-range defence but not suited to long voyages.

The Armada sailed up the Channel in a great crescent.

✿ Why do you think the Spanish fleet sailed in a formation like this?

The two fleets first sighted one another on 21 July and fought for over a week. The English ships had more cannon and used their better firepower to hit and run, but failed to stop the Armada sailing up the Channel. The Spanish ships carried over 18,000 troops, but could not get close enough to board the English ships and capture them.

Tudor sea battles often ended with hand-to-hand fighting. War with the Spanish lasted for years after the defeat of the Armada. Here, Sir Richard Grenville fights a last ditch battle against overwhelming odds.

The Armada reached Calais only to find that their extra troops had not arrived. On the night of 28 July the English attacked with fire-ships and forced the Spanish to cut anchors and scatter. In the Battle of Gravelines, the next day, the merciless navy pounced on any Spanish ships they found sailing alone.

Bad weather stopped the remaining ships in the Armada joining forces once more. Storms then drove the Spanish northwards. Many were wrecked as they struggled to sail home round Scotland and Ireland. England was saved!

Your project

By now you should be fully armed with facts about Tudor warfare. This is the time to think about the sort of project you might like to produce.

One of the most exciting aspects of Tudor times is the gallery of amazing heroes who lived and fought through these dangerous years. Try writing a short life story or biography. Here are a few suggestions:

- The Earl of Essex was just 20 when the ageing Queen Elizabeth fell for his charms. But how did war in Ireland lead them to quarrel?
- Sir Walter Raleigh was Elizabeth's most trusted courtier, but he was executed in 1618 by James I. Why did he fall from royal favour?
- Mary, Queen of Scots was held prisoner by Elizabeth for many years. Was she really a traitor?
- James IV was the young and bold king of Scotland. Was he foolish to help the French against Henry VIII in 1513?

Remember, this is your project, so choose someone who interests you.

The young and attractive Earl of Essex.

Project Presentation
- Research your hero. Use the Internet and your local library. Is there a society, museum or historic site connected to your hero?
- If you were a time-travelling journalist and could interview your hero or heroine, what questions would you ask him or her? Make a list, and then see if you can answer them from your research.
- Collect pictures showing different aspects of your hero or heroine's life. Use them to illustrate your biography.

Mary, Queen of Scots was beheaded for plotting with the Spanish to overthrow Queen Elizabeth I.

Sherlock Bones has been finding out about Queen Elizabeth's bold sea-dogs. This was a nickname for her best and most daring sailors. He really liked the story of Sir Richard Grenville. In 1591, Sir Richard and the crew of his ship, the *Revenge*, fought a lone battle against at least fifteen Spanish warships. After fifteen hours' fighting they surrendered. Sir Richard later died of his wounds.

Look out for other bold sea-dogs, such as Sebastian Cabot, Martin Frobisher and Sir John Hawkins – they would make great subjects for your project too.

A Tudor galleon.

Glossary

apprentice A young person learning a skilled trade.

armada A great fleet, especially of Spain.

artillery Large guns and cannon.

bastion The pointed part of a fort.

bill-man A soldier who fought with a bill – a weapon that could be used as a spear, hook and axe.

Catholic A member of the Roman Catholic Church, ruled by the Pope in Rome.

fire-ship A ship that was set on fire before being sailed towards the enemy's vessels.

ligature A cord used to tie up a bleeding artery.

Lord Lieutenant The official in charge of the county militia, usually a trusted noble.

marches Border districts.

monarch A king or queen.

musketeer A soldier who fought with a musket – a gun with a long barrel.

the Netherlands Another name for Holland.

noble A member of the aristocracy.

Protestants A Christian belonging to the Protestant Church.

pulley block A simple machine used to lift heavy weights easily.

rebellion An attempt to overthrow the monarch using force.

recruit A new soldier.

shipwright A craftsman who designed and built ships.

standard A flag.

wardens Local governors who had to enforce the law.

weevils Insects which lived in ship's biscuits.

Answers

page 4

❀ As well as being a ferocious mythical beast, the red dragon is the symbol of Wales.

page 7

❀ Beggars made up many of the foot soldiers fighting abroad in Elizabethan times. They could become good soldiers if they were led well, but they were hardly ideal!

page 9

❀ Some diseases were spread through infected water. Beer was often drunk because it was cleaner and safer than water. But alcohol was also a way of cheering soldiers up!

Page 11

❀ English longbows needed great strength and accuracy to hit and penetrate a target. Archers were like trained athletes today – the more they practised, the better they became. The government even tried to pass laws against playing games like football – because they stopped boys concentrating on archery.

page 12

❀ Bows, cannon, swords, bills, muskets, pikes.

page 15

❀ The best Tudor surgeons learnt their skills treating wounded soldiers on the battlefields.

page 17

❀ Reiver: An old word for robber or bandit.

❀ Blackmail: Now it means demanding payment to keep quiet about a secret. To the Reivers it meant demanding protection money. *Pay up or we raid your farm!*

page 19

✤ This was a joke, because it was so big. It was like calling Robin Hood's large friend 'Little John'.

page 21

✤ *Weapons and ammunition:* cannon, handguns, gunpowder, powder scoops and flasks, shot; bows and arrows; pikes and bills; swords.
Food: biscuits, beer, salted meat and fish; dried peas; flour.
Navigation equipment: lead sounding weights to measure water depth; sand glass, compass; protractor, log and reel to measure speed.
Sails and rigging: spare canvas and rope; needles and threads, pulley blocks (a big ship needed a thousand of these).
Domestic life: wooden bowls, spoons, cooking pots; candle lanterns, clothes, books, games, musical instruments; grindstones for sharpening knives; surgeons' instruments.

page 22

✤ They have been described like this: cold, a little crunchy, tasting a bit like calves' foot jelly. Yummy!

page 24

✤ It means greatness from small beginnings. Drake was proud, though very sensitive about his humble origins. His motto showed how much he had achieved in life.

page 26

✤ The Spanish ships grouped together to protect themselves. Poorly armed ships sailed in the centre, protected by two 'horns' of warships.

Books to read

Look Inside a Tudor Warship
by Brian Moses (Hodder Wayland, 2002)

Elizabeth I and the Armada
by John Guy (Ticktock, 1999)

All About the Tudors
by Heather Morris (Hodder Wayland, 2001)

Who? What? When? The Tudors
by Bob Fowke (Hodder Wayland, 2003)

Places to visit

Bosworth Battlefield Visitor Centre and Country Park
Sutton Cheney
Nuneaton
Warwickshire
CV13 OAD

Deal Castle
Deal
Kent

Elizabethan Walls
Berwick-on-Tweed
Northumberland

Index